THE VIRTUAL TEAMS POCKETBOOK

By Ian Fleming

Drawings by Phil Hailstone

"Insightful and thought provoking – a must read for prospective virtual team leaders and members in today's rapid global economy."

James Mullican
President, Advanced Waste Management Systems Inc., USA

"Tie it to your desk, don't lend it to a friend, this is such a valuable resource that you will never see it again. If you have to plan and manage a virtual team this is the book you have been waiting for."

Ray Sleeman
Director, The Tourism and Leisure Group Ltd, New Zealand

Published by:
Management Pocketbooks Ltd
Laurel House, Station Approach, Alresford, Hants SO24 9JH, U.K.
Tel: +44 (0)1962 735573   Fax: +44 (0)1962 733637
E-mail: sales@pocketbook.co.uk
Website: www.pocketbook.co.uk

This edition published 2006.

British Library Cataloguing-in-Publication Data – A catalogue record for this book is available from the British Library.

ISBN-13   978 1 903776 41 4
ISBN-10   1 903776 41 4

Design, typesetting and graphics by **efex ltd**. Printed in U.K.

CONTENTS

 WHAT IS A VIRTUAL TEAM? 5
Outline, definitions, ways of working, examples, what's in a name?, development of virtual teams, potential, dangerous assumptions

 WHERE TO START – TEAM LEADERS 19
Questions to ask, what is leadership?, what makes a leader?, skills you will need, how should you lead?, selecting your team

 WHERE TO START – TEAM MEMBERS 35
Virtual teamworking – is it for you?, what's your experience?, can you deliver?, any questions?

 CULTURE & TEAMS 45
What is culture?, ways people differ, culture in the workplace, the challenge for VTs, team members from different organisations and countries, want to know more?

 LEARNING TO WORK TOGETHER 55
The effect of distance, good meeting practice, agree ways of working, build up a knowledge bank, talk through cultural issues, making the most of your meetings

 BUILDING TRUST 67
The big challenge, issues for virtual teams, necessary behaviours, demonstrating trust, positive steps, 'swift trust'

 MAKING TECHNOLOGY WORK FOR YOU 77
Where are you starting from?, the purpose of technology, real time and asynchronous, instant messaging, whiteboards, audio conferencing, video conferencing, email, your own virtual community, role of a moderator, discussion boards, file and web sharing, summary

 FINAL THOUGHTS 105
Lead, don't manage, don't run away from conflict, communication, it's all about people

FURTHER READING 110

The term <u>virtual team</u> started to appear in the language of organisations during the 1990s.

While both the benefits and skills of team working have been known for many years, a new type of team is now evolving. A team often put together using the best skills available, across a range of locations, organisations or continents – yet one that may never meet.

Virtual teams (VTs) weren't planned, they simply evolved. With the advances in technology, the globalisation of business and the need to create products in shorter time pressures, new ways of working started to develop.

Virtual teams are now reshaping the way we think and do business. What's more we are learning as we go along: research data on the topic is only just emerging.

It's an exciting and challenging new area. As you will see, it's not simply about technology but a way of thinking and operating that takes us to a different level.

Ian Fleming

WHAT IS A VIRTUAL TEAM?

OUTLINE OF THE BOOK

This book is aimed at both team leaders and members.
In it you will find information and ideas on:

- The whole area of virtual teams, what they are and how they evolved

- Where to start, with suggestions for leaders and team members

- Culture and its potential effect on teams

- Learning to work together

- Ways of developing trust – a big issue for virtual teams, and

- Making technology work for you

WHAT IS A VIRTUAL TEAM?

DEFINITIONS

You may have difficulty in finding the term *virtual team* in a dictionary. Taken separately the words mean:

Virtual: Existing or resulting in essence or effect though not in actual fact, form, or name.

Team: A number of people who co-operate in such a way that they achieve more than the sum total of the individual's efforts.
A group of people working together to achieve a common goal.

A frequently used description that would seem to embrace both these definitions is:

Working together apart.

WHAT IS A VIRTUAL TEAM?

DEFINITIONS

A virtual team (VT) is:

- A collection of people physically separated by geography, location and/or time
- A network of people who are able to work together and interact using advances in technology
- Often temporary in nature, consisting of people with a range of skills and experiences who work in different locations to achieve a specific task in a set time period
- Not always 100% virtual and may sometimes meet

VIRTUAL WAYS OF WORKING

Virtual teamworking allows your team to be in touch with each other when working at:

- Different times in different places
- The same time in different places
- Different times in the same place
- The same time in the same place
- Any time and in any place

EXAMPLES OF VIRTUAL TEAMS

Virtual teams can occur in all types of organisations from small businesses to large multinationals. A few examples are:

Sales teams: In a variety of businesses/industries operating across the country, who share information about customers, competition and the marketplace. They mostly communicate by phone and email and sometimes get together for sales meetings.

Aircraft design: Both Boeing and Airbus have set up teams of designers, engineers, suppliers and customers to develop their new range of aircraft. In this type of VT, team leaders often manage people who don't work for their company.

Events: Run annually across the country. Throughout the year a team of designers, suppliers, trade associations and venue staff are in touch to plan what needs to be done.

WHAT IS A VIRTUAL TEAM?

WHAT'S IN A NAME?

There are a number of terms used to describe teams that work virtually, eg:

Cyber or network teams do most of their business using electronic technology rather than meeting.

Global/geographically dispersed teams – people working in different locations, who are tasked with achieving a business-related project.

Business improvement teams develop recommendations for improving a process or systems.

Service teams such as call centres supporting customers 24 hours a day.

Action teams respond to emergency situations.

It's not only about work, however. 'Teams' based on friendship and mutual interests, and professional groups who share knowledge and experiences, often use technology and operate virtually.

DEVELOPMENT OF VIRTUAL TEAMS

Businesses have changed:

- While organisations have always operated in different locations, people are increasingly being asked to work together across locations and share responsibility for a product or outcome
- Global corporations have emerged, spanning a range of industries or services operating globally 24 hours a day, 7 days a week on different continents and across time zones
- Customers' requirements mean that pressure is on to deliver products to market, often within tight deadlines
- Relationships with customers, suppliers and stakeholders are increasingly based on co-operation and collaboration
- Strategic alliances and partnerships have become more common

DEVELOPMENT OF VIRTUAL TEAMS

Knowledge is key:

- Knowledge is possibly the most important resource for the new economy
- As organisations have downsized they have discovered that they have also lost a lot of their knowledge
- Knowledge management and experience are crucial to meet the challenge of tackling the increasing complexity of today's products and product cycles
- While knowledge will always be a source of power, the emphasis now is on sharing what we know both within the whole organisation and, where appropriate, with others, rather than keeping it to ourselves
- Knowledge is, however, only useful if you do something with it

DEVELOPMENT OF VIRTUAL TEAMS

People factors:

- Organisations face a shortage of skills together with a rise in employment costs
- It's expensive to send people off to different locations for meetings and visits
- Technology has created the opportunity and the means to communicate with anyone in the world 24 hours a day, at the touch of a button/keyboard
- People are beginning to make lifestyle choices about:
    - what they want to do with their lives
    - how and where they want to work
    - where they want to live, *and*
    - often show a reluctance to move for the sake of a job or an organisation

POTENTIAL OF VIRTUAL TEAMS

Virtual teams hold out the possibilities of:

- Recruiting talent and using the best brains and resources **irrespective of where they are based or who they work for**
- Achieving major breakthroughs quicker and more cost effectively
- Saving money and time on travel and accommodation
- Building a new set of working relationships within and outside organisations
- Presenting new learning opportunities to team leaders and team members
- Challenging the way business is carried out and offering new ways of working as:
  - old style hierarchies and power bases are collapsing
  - networking becomes more important
  - leadership is based on a person's strengths, not their seniority, job title or how long they have been with the organisation

DANGEROUS ASSUMPTIONS

1: Virtual teams are like normal teams with people based in different places

- This has some truth but much of what we know about teams is based on learning gained in face to face situations; **virtual teams present different challenges**
- While all teams need leaders and goals, and an effective way of working, VTs face the task of building unity within a group of people who may never meet and who work across time zones
- Don't make the mistake of simply transferring what you know about teams to these new virtual situations – a lot more is involved

DANGEROUS ASSUMPTIONS

2: *Virtual teams are all about technology*

- Technology plays a major part in how teams **operate**, but success comes from applying inspirational leadership, developing trust, blending the skills available and encouraging both participation and accountability

- The human skills of getting people to co-operate and work together are key, not just using technology

DANGEROUS ASSUMPTIONS

3:   Virtual teams will always work if they have the best people

- No team is guaranteed success. Even selecting the best players does not necessarily ensure that you'll be successful

- Teams fall short of their potential for many reasons, from setting unrealistic goals and expectations, to a failure of members to engage with the leader

- Many VTs have people from different countries and cultures. If the challenges this presents are not recognised and allowed for, then the team is likely to hit problems

Virtual teams can be effective and this book shows how. However, don't underestimate the thought that needs to go into getting the team together and making it work.

WHERE TO START –
<u>TEAM LEADERS</u>

WHERE TO START – TEAM LEADERS

QUESTIONS TO ASK

All teams, face to face or virtual, need leaders – someone to set the direction, get people involved and inspire them to give of their best. If you've been asked to lead a VT it pays to find the answers to the following questions:

What exactly is the brief: what have you been asked to do and why?
For example, are you expected to lead a team that's:

- Developing a product or service from scratch for a new market

- Working on a project, eg the introduction of a new business process or system

- Using people from across the organisation to look at better ways of working

- Organising an event by pulling in people from different locations, companies, interest groups

- Sharing a range of experiences around a particular topic such as medical research, social trends, best practice, etc

The words *virtual team* may not have been mentioned at this stage. It's only when you start to think through what is involved that you realise the implications of the task ahead.

QUESTIONS TO ASK

What's the bigger picture?
- Find out what else might be happening within your organisation or outside and where your team fits
- Remember that activities rarely happen in isolation

Who are the stakeholders?
- Who has a share or an interest in making sure that your team is successful?
- These people may not be noticeable at first, so you may have to do some research to find out who they are

What will 'success' look like?
- It is a leader's job to create a vision to inspire others
- Asking this question early on will help you create a picture of what this might look like

QUESTIONS TO ASK

What timescales are you working towards?
- In today's fast-paced world you may have limited time available
- This could have implications for how you run your team, especially if quick results are needed

What resources are available?
- The list should include people, information, equipment, materials, premises as well as time and money
- Many of these may well be hard to come by or not thought through

Who's available to join the team?
- Names may be mentioned of people you do not know
- It's not unusual for those nominated not to know that their names have been put forward!

Why does this matter?

These are basic questions that any person chosen to lead a team should be asking.

If you don't know where you're starting from, how will you know you are heading in the right direction?

QUESTIONS TO ASK YOURSELF

Why have you been chosen as team leader?
- Is it because of your position, experience, particular expertise, contacts or that you were the only person available?

What experience do you have of leading others?
- You could have been a leader at work, in your leisure time (in a club or society) or at home

What do you know about leadership?
- Think of your own experiences of leading and of being led by others.
  What lessons have you learnt about what to do and what not to do?

Why does this matter?

Leadership is the key to any successful team. In a virtual setting it becomes even more important when leading people who may never meet and who you don't really know. If your first leadership role is with a virtual team, you could find it more demanding than expected.

WHAT IS LEADERSHIP?

- In simple terms leadership is about **getting people to follow you: achieving goals with the support of others**

- We *all* have the ability to lead people: in work situations, from a distance, in a family situation or in our spare time in a voluntary capacity

- Leadership is not about following a manual, a set of rules or trying to be like others. It's about developing your own unique way of leading, one that convinces others to follow you

WHAT MAKES A LEADER?

Writers on leadership have their own views on the skills effective leaders need to have. However, ask staff to identify the *best leadership* characteristics of their bosses and they will talk about them being:

- Creative and visionary – yet realistic
- Inspirational motivators – encouraging people to go even further
- Able to learn from mistakes and failures
- Willing to take risks but also having a plan
- Firm, clear-cut and decisive
- Highly driven, with a desire to achieve excellence
- Able to develop loyalty by investing in relationships
- Sociable, friendly, warm, supportive and approachable
- Willing to put group interests ahead of their own
- Able to strike the right balance between people and results

WHAT MAKES A LEADER?

You'll need many, if not all, of these skills when leading a virtual team.

Problems faced when leading from a distance and across time zones can have greater impact simply because you are not around to handle the situation.

For example, if you are experiencing communication difficulties – whether language problems, breakdowns in technology or people failing to meet deadlines – quick action is needed to maintain relationships as well as productivity and focus.

The following pages set out the particular skills that VT leaders need, based on my experience of working with a wide range of virtual teams.

SKILLS YOU WILL NEED

Competent at leading teams – with a track record of achieving results. You need to be able to inspire people (often strangers) with a vision and encourage others to share in your passion.

Self-aware – know your strengths and limitations. In a virtual team context, when leading from a distance, you need to know when to let go and when to ask for help. Leadership is not about knowing all the answers.

Proactive – able to spot what's happening – or failing to happen – and take appropriate action. People will let you down and not meet their commitments. For example, team members will often say *'yes'* to requests simply because it's against their culture to say *'no'*.

Persuasive and influential – able to form relationships with people you may not know, and with whom you have limited contact, in a way that inspires them to want to take part.

SKILLS YOU WILL NEED

Credible and able to build trust – trust is one of the main issues in virtual teams. If people do not have confidence in you as a person or in what you do then you will struggle to make progress.

Politically astute – able to manoeuvre your way round an organisation (yours and others) to get the resources and support needed for success.

Culturally aware – VTs often have people from different locations, organisations and countries. Each has their own culture or way of working. The skill of recognising and dealing effectively with these differences – and build a team around them – is vital for a leader.

Assertive – able to use a range of assertive responses to situations that may arise in order to get a win-win result for the team.

SKILLS YOU WILL NEED

Technically competent, but not technically obsessed – there's an increasing range of technology available to help VTs to communicate, share and keep in touch. Knowing what's available and how to use it effectively is crucial, as is identifying when it's **not** the answer to the problem.

Skilled communicator – leading from a distance calls for the ability to present ideas and thoughts clearly, using a variety of methods, and to listen accurately to the responses.

Good at networking – the skilled leader will actively use and encourage networking within the team and wider community. Getting things done can be more about who you know than what you know.

Effective coach and mentor – these are more challenging skills when carried out from a distance, using audio, video and online communication.

SKILLS YOU WILL NEED

Good at project management – if the VT is
set up to develop a product or make
recommendations then view it as a
project. Project management involves:

- A definite beginning and end
- Using various tools to measure
  activities and track tasks
- Calling upon resources as and when needed

As with projects, VTs have to deliver results that are:

- On time
- Within cost and scope
- To a standard and quality required
  by the customer

SKILLS YOU WILL NEED

Project management also involves:

- Leading
- Planning the work of others
- People management
- Communication
- Negotiating
- Problem solving and creativity

Project managers aim to create an environment and conditions in which a clear goal can be achieved by a team of people.

Virtual team leaders do all this – *from a distance.*

Why does this matter?

It's essential that you appreciate the range of skills you will need. If people in your VT don't get direction and help it is easy for them to drop out, claiming that they are wasting their time. This could make your team's task almost impossible.

Should you feel that you need help to develop any of these leadership skills, start looking sooner rather than later. Be honest about your abilities or you may find yourself exposed at a later stage.

HOW SHOULD YOU LEAD?

In a face to face team it is possible, with a lot of effort, to achieve success by creating loyalty and commitment to the task as well as to colleagues.

In VTs, people's primary loyalty is likely to be **to themselves and their own organisation**. This could affect what you are trying to do and create within your team.

For example, don't expect:

- That people will necessarily stay for the duration of a project – specialists tend to be busy and in demand
- That your team will be a perfect mix of team types (eg Belbin roles) – people may have been chosen for their skills and availability, or even for political reasons, rather than for their styles
- That your team members will automatically be interested in attempts to develop their personal skills and relationships with others. They may see it simply as another job

HOW SHOULD YOU LEAD?

If you can encourage people to work together and tap into what they know and can do, then potentially you have the basis for creating something special.

Be prepared to wear many hats and to fulfil a hands-on role by:

- Shaping the direction and energy of the team
- Focusing on **performance** and **outputs** as opposed to processes (how things are done)
- Encouraging people to share their ideas, thoughts and suggestions
- Making people accountable for deliverables and deadlines
- Sharing leadership where appropriate, yet retaining overall control
- Making things happen 'behind the scenes' to ensure that the team has the resources to operate and is not held back by politics or red tape
- Keeping in regular contact with individuals, both to monitor contributions and performance, and to check how people are feeling

SELECTING YOUR TEAM

In an ideal world you would be able to pick the best available people for your team. In reality you usually have to go with whoever is available or even who is the cheapest to employ. The test of your ability is how well you blend people of different skills and experiences into an effective team.

Even though your choices may be limited, try to influence who joins. Given the special requirements of working virtually, it will pay you to invest time talking to potential team members. Be prepared to question people beforehand about what they can bring to the team. See pages 40 - 43 for questions they may ask you and give some thought to how to answer them.

Why does this matter?

Problems frequently emerge in teams (eg quality of work, level of skills and people's availability) that could have been highlighted earlier. In your initial discussions you are looking for reassurance that they can cope, deliver what's required and not let you and the team down.

WHERE TO START –
<u>TEAM MEMBERS</u>

VIRTUAL TEAMWORKING – IS IT FOR YOU?

Your reaction to being invited to join a team could range from pleasure at being selected to frustration at the extra demands. It's not unusual for others to put your name forward without even letting you know.

Perhaps the idea of virtual teamworking does not appeal or suit your preferred way of operating. For example, you may prefer:

- To know your colleagues and be able to discuss any problems face to face
- To be in the traditional office situation that offers a degree of comfort, routine and friendship. One in which you know how things work

Successful virtual teamworking requires you to be a self-starter, able to deliver goals on time, and work independently and unsupervised. You need to be willing to open up to relative strangers and share your knowledge and ideas. Not everybody wants or is able to do this. If you are one of these people, then speak up now.

WHAT'S YOUR EXPERIENCE?

If the idea of working in a virtual team appeals to you, then consider what you can offer as well as any questions you may have.

Think about your experience of working in teams:

- What projects were the teams working on?
- What roles did you play?
- How successful were those teams – what made them successful?
- What problems did the teams face and how were they handled?
- How would you describe the leaders you worked under?
- What do you look for in a leader?
- What is your experience of leading others?

WHAT'S YOUR EXPERIENCE?

- Have you ever worked in a virtual team and/or a virtual environment?
- How did you get on; what was it like?
- In what ways was it different from a face to face team?
- What experience have you had of using:
  - instant messaging
  - whiteboard
  - audio conferencing
  - video conferencing
  - email
  - discussion board
  - file share
  - web share?
- In what ways did you use these technologies and what lessons did you learn?

CAN YOU DELIVER?

Think about the knowledge, skills and experiences you can offer any team.
In addition you'll be asked to give both time and commitment.

The chances are that you may also have other jobs to do in addition to working
in this new team. In fact you may already belong to several teams. This is not
uncommon given that you are good at your job or have knowledge and skills
that are in demand.

Give some thought to what working in a new team will do to any existing
workload – how will you balance the various demands?

If there are any potential problems or conflicts, then it pays to be honest (with
yourself and others) and raise them sooner rather than later.

ANY QUESTIONS?

As a potential team member, you are likely to have many concerns and questions that you will hope your team leader can answer. For example:

Why have I been chosen?
Often because of a particular skill or experience that makes you good at what you do. The downside of this is that you could also be involved in other initiatives, everybody wanting your time and contribution.

Will I be full time in this team or expected to do it as part of my existing job(s)?
You want to know where you stand and how much commitment of time and effort you will be expected to make. If you are needed full time there will be implications for your existing job, eg can you be released and who covers your job?

What's in it for me?
A fair question. If you are asked to give up your time and effort, you might be expecting something in return. In addition, there are wider implications such as, will it help or hinder your career progression?

ANY QUESTIONS?

To whom will I report?
Membership of a VT could mean that you have at least
two bosses, the team leader and a functional one. It pays
to find out to whom you will be reporting. Failure to do so
can cause confusion and problems.

How will I be appraised and who will do it?
Normally your boss does your appraisal. Who will
do it in the future and what issues might that raise?

What are the implications for my pay?
You may currently receive a bonus on top of your
regular salary as part of your employment package.
Will this still be the case? In reality, how will people be
rewarded for their contributions to the virtual team?

ANY QUESTIONS?

Why should I give away my expertise to others?
If you are nominated for your abilities and experience, you may be reluctant to give away your hard-won knowledge and expertise to strangers.

What if it all goes wrong?
While you hope that the VT will not fail, things do not always go according to plan. Should this happen, it is right to ask who'll carry the can and get the blame.

How will we communicate and keep in touch?
This is a potential problem for teams based in the same building as well as for those located across continents. It raises questions around:
- technology that will be used (are the systems compatible?)
- skill levels of team members (could language be a problem?) and ...
- timescales if the team is spread out across different zones.

ANY QUESTIONS?

Why should I follow you as a leader?
You may find that you have more knowledge and experience than the chosen leader. You may well not know them or even work in the same organisation. You might want to seek reassurance that the leader is credible and shares your beliefs and ways of working.

How are we going to work together?
Look for examples of **practical** ideas that will be used for building relationships and keeping people in touch.

What role do you want me to play?
You need to know at the start what is expected of you and what you will be responsible for delivering.

ANY QUESTIONS?

 What will happen when it's all over? Frequently, VTs are set up to achieve a specific task in a period of time. While this can be both challenging and demanding, it can also create potential problems when the job is finished. For example, when you return to your own organisation, at what level do you go back? What happens to the people who have been doing the work in your absence?

Why does this matter?

Clearing up individual concerns and potential issues at the start can save valuable time and effort.

Culture & Teams

WHAT IS CULTURE?

Culture is the way we do things. It's how we behave as individuals and in groups. This is, however, far too simple an explanation. It is more useful to regard culture as referring to shared assumptions, beliefs, values, norms and actions.

Culture is shaped by our experiences in a wide variety of situations that influence the way we view and understand the world in which we live. These past experiences, often handed down from generation to generation, influence:

- Our values: what we consider attractive and unattractive
- What is and is not acceptable behaviour
- What is right and wrong
- How we interpret the world

WHAT IS CULTURE?

When we refer to 'a culture' we are talking about a group of people who share a similar background. This often shows itself in hidden patterns of communication, viewpoints they adopt and expressions that they use.

These hidden patterns have an effect on the way people behave, how they see the world and work with others. Taken together they can form what is collectively known as a *cultural pattern*.

The danger with cultural patterns is that they can lead us to stereotyping and making generalisations about professions, people and nationalities.

Examples are emerging of expensive failures when organisations have tried to bring people together in virtual teams from different cultures. While the business objective may be valid, the problems that arise are usually related to lack of skill at working with cross-cultural groups.

WAYS PEOPLE DIFFER

Visible cultural differences include:

- Communication styles – open or closed
- Response to conflict – avoid or confront
- Approaches to completing tasks – deadline driven or 'whenever'
- Decision making styles – consensus or 'refer to the most senior'
- Willingness to disclose information or feelings – open or secretive

Invisible cultural roots that influence behaviour are people's:

- Beliefs
- Values
- Perceptions
- Expectations
- Attitudes
- Assumptions

(See: www.1000ventures.com for more on managing cultural differences)

CULTURE IN THE WORKPLACE

Each organisation has its own culture which may vary from site to site, location to location, country to country.

Occupational groups develop work cultures in the same way as people from different countries. For example, the Marketing department may have different ways of expressing ideas and views from people working in Finance.

In building teams from the same country, we might have a good idea as to what motivates people and how they may react to certain situations. As a result we can work at creating the conditions for them to perform (though that's not to say that this is easy).

If your team includes people from different countries, it may only be when trying to make sense of their behaviours that you realise what you don't know.

THE CHALLENGE FOR VTs

Working with others from different countries, companies and disciplines brings definite advantages. The potential exists for new ways of looking at challenges, generating ideas and improving working relationships.

This needs to be balanced against the reality that virtual teams are rarely formed as a deliberate way of promoting better methods of working. They usually come about because particular people with specific expertise are required, regardless of where they are based.

In practice, a great deal of time can be spent in promoting understanding and getting people to work effectively together. Those teams that succeed have thought through the cultural, technological and organisational issues and worked out ways of dealing with them.

As with many initiatives, **planning and education** are the keys to success.

THE CHALLENGE FOR VTS

Why does this matter?

- If your team comprises people from different locations or organisations, there's a good chance that cultural differences will exist. Your team needs to recognise this and take account of the implications for the way that you will operate

- People from different countries and cultures will have their own view of the world and ways of doing things. (As an example, try asking each person to define 'team' and see what you get.) When setting up your virtual team, it's easy to overlook this and assume that we're all the same. In so doing, you may unknowingly cause great offence to others

- All cultures are complex and contain an element of generalisation – it is easy to assume these to be 'fact' with little or no evidence to back it up

- So, when working with other cultures it pays to stop and consider what assumptions you are making. How valid are they? Check them out and, if necessary, make adjustments

CULTURE & TEAMS

TEAM MEMBERS FROM DIFFERENT ORGANISATIONS

In the early days of your team, it is worth having a conversation around the culture of the organisation from which people have come, exploring such topics as:

- How work is organised and authority given to people
- How people are recognised and rewarded for their work
- What the organisation values and how that is demonstrated
- The usual management style
- The scope for initiative, risk-taking and individuality
- How decisions are made and by whom
- How differences in status show themselves
- How teams are organised and run
- The type of leadership they see demonstrated
- How ideas and suggestions are encouraged

This will give you a picture of people's expectations and how they have been used to working.

TEAM MEMBERS FROM DIFFERENT COUNTRIES

If you know that you will have a multi-cultural team, then John Mattock's excellent *Cross-cultural Business Pocketbook* offers the following guidelines:

1. Appreciate and enjoy cultural diversity, accepting that your own perceptions are coloured by upbringing within your native culture.
2. Try to empathise with the other person's views.
3. Do some homework to understand the background better. Be open-minded – don't dump a national sterotype on individuals.
4. Work at developing trust and then openly discuss how respective cultural differences might be affecting an issue.
5. Begin in a formal, polite manner and await signals of informality from the other person.
6. Recognise the extra stress imposed by language barriers and make allowances for others without appearing patronising.
7. On vital matters always double-check understanding to avoid expensive mistakes.
8. Plan any communication to eliminate the negative and build on the positive. Simple, clear, direct, honest and open are the best styles for communication across cultures.

WANT TO KNOW MORE?

The whole area of working with people from different cultures is fascinating and growing in importance. The following authors are widely quoted in this context:

Geert Hofstede's work on cultural dimensions is probably the most popular in the area of cultural research. Although the work provides a relatively general framework for analysis, it can be applied easily to many everyday intercultural encounters. www.geert-hofstede.com

Fons Trompenaars and his colleagues have detailed their research in a string of books, of which *Riding the Waves of Culture* (Nicholas Brealey Publishing) and *Building Cross-cultural Competence* (John Wiley & Sons) stand out. www.thtconsulting.com

For tips on communication technology for global virtual teams look up www.diversophy.com. They look at various methods such as emails, teleconferences and their implications for the cultures described by Hofstede.

When Cultures Collide by Richard D. Lewis (Nicholas Brealey Publishing) provides insights into global businesses.

LEARNING TO WORK TOGETHER

THE EFFECT OF DISTANCE

When you are planning how your team will communicate and work together, bear in mind the impact that distance has on both communications, collaboration and productivity.

Professor Tom Allen of Massachusetts Institute of Technology conducted extensive research over many years into the relationship between distance and the level of regular communication between people. His research revealed a clear link between distance and **frequency** of communication. For example, if there's a distance of more than 50 feet (15+ metres) between people, the probability of them communicating and co-operating more than once a week was quoted at less than 10%.

The radius for collaborative co-operation therefore is very small.

LEARNING TO WORK TOGETHER

THE EFFECT OF DISTANCE

Tom Allen's work has implications if you are, for example:

- A team based in the same location but geographically spread out on different floors or even in different buildings

- Doing a field based job that involves spending most of your time out of the office, yet being expected to share ideas and information on a regular basis

- Part of a VT that includes people from as far apart as Asia and the west coast of America. Working across time zones can lead to a very short 'window' when everyone is available for conference calls.

It might also help to explain why mistakes happen, communications break down and opportunities are missed within teams.

GOOD MEETING PRACTICE

If the team is to be successful, then it pays to meet face to face at the start to:

- Get to know each other and build relationships
- Talk through the task and work out the best ways of tackling it
- Set ground rules for the team and work out how you will operate
- Agree on ways of communicating and any technology to use
- Carry out any necessary training (eg technical, cultural, product)
- Talk about trust and how it can be demonstrated in the team
- Plan the next steps

Whatever the financial and logistical difficulties, it's worth the leader making the strongest possible case to hold a meeting, and individuals making every effort to attend. As a team you will have a difficult job trusting each other if you have not met.

If you can get together, then the meeting needs careful planning as well as enough time to cover all the necessary areas.

LEARNING TO WORK TOGETHER

GOOD MEETING PRACTICE

If you are the team leader arranging the first team meeting:

- Work out what you **need** to cover
- Use any information gained from one to one meetings with potential team members to help you plan
- Break down any grand statements into **practical** actions and timescales for discussion
- Arrange to demonstrate any technology the team will be using **and allow time for practice**
- Create space within the timetable for people to get to know each other
- Think through what questions and issues are likely to be raised (have some answers ready), as well as what could go wrong
- Create your communications around visual displays that will help convey meaning across different cultures
- Invite all those involved in the team – including core team members, key support people, stakeholders/sponsors
- Enlist help (or certainly seek advice) from a skilled facilitator if needed

LEARNING TO WORK TOGETHER

GOOD MEETING PRACTICE

At your meeting:

- Be prepared to share information not only about your work but also about your family, hobbies and interests

- Pick up on topics of mutual interest that you hear others talking about. This is a useful way of developing your skills, especially if you are not confident in speaking the language

- Think about recording personal information about your fellow team members and publishing it on the team's website (see pages 97-98 for ideas)

- Build up a map showing where everyone is based

- Invite key people to spend some time, formally and informally, with your group. Top management support is critical. There's nothing worse than the five minute cameo from the top person who is then never seen again

LEARNING TO WORK TOGETHER

GOOD MEETING PRACTICE

As a team keep in mind:

- What has to be achieved – expressing it visually is a useful way of helping people understand and remain focused
- How what you are doing fits into the bigger picture and other initiatives
- The needs of the stakeholders plus any quality standards that you may have set
- The budget to which you are working
- Key dates and timescales, etc

LEARNING TO WORK TOGETHER

AGREE WAYS OF WORKING

It's important that as a team you work out the details of how you are going to operate.
Ideas include:

- Inviting people's suggestions and experiences – especially if they have had previous experience of working in a virtual team. Try and build on what has worked for people and learn from what did not

- Drawing up a clear project plan that involves all the team in the details of what needs to happen to make it a success

- Agreeing some ground rules for the team

- Identifying roles and responsibilities – who does what

- Deciding how you're going to communicate as a team, both formally and informally

LEARNING TO WORK TOGETHER

AGREE WAYS OF WORKING

Further suggestions include:

- Establishing norms for responding to phone calls, emails, checking message boards, etc

- Deciding on ways of sharing information and dealing with problems; how decisions should be made and conflict handled

- Working on agreeing a common language

- Clarifying timescales, setting priorities and deadlines

- Working out ways of reviewing progress

- Talking openly about any concerns that you might have, and in particular what could go wrong

As your team develops, be prepared to review how you are working and make changes if necessary.

LEARNING TO WORK TOGETHER

BUILD UP A KNOWLEDGE BANK

Research reveals that people who operate well in virtual teams are willing to share and exchange information. In each team you will have a wealth of knowledge available before you even start. This needs to be shared and built up as the team develops.

- Think about putting together a skills/competency database as well as a network of contacts

- Each of you will have your own way of working that will probably include how you use technology. Is there anything that you could learn from this as a team?

- As your team develops, start to include *'What have we learnt?'* in any meetings (face to face and/or online) that you hold and record what emerges

- Bear in mind that what you create as a team is potentially more valuable than any training course or textbook, as it comes from your own shared experiences

LEARNING TO WORK TOGETHER

TALK THROUGH CULTURAL ISSUES

If you are part of a multicultural team, then use it as an opportunity to learn about the other nationalities and how they do business. Consider specialist training if it would help your team work better at understanding each other.

Try to learn some very simple phrases in the languages of your fellow team members. Having done so, get in the habit of using them when you meet either face to face or online.

When working virtually it will soon become apparent just how differently people around the world think, live and work. However, learning to adapt to different cultures immediately is not easy.

Remember that because somebody does not speak your language as well as you, it does not mean that they are any less capable. Although they may not do business in the same way as you, that's not to say that they are wrong. Be patient with them.

MAKING THE MOST OF YOUR MEETINGS

Why does this matter?

As a team you need to create an environment and way of working that will help you succeed. Everyone has a part to play in making this happen. Getting people together is the best – and possibly only – chance you will all have of making a good start.

Meetings, handled skilfully, can have many potential benefits, with the sharing of ideas and experiences as well as networking opportunities. More importantly, they are a way of getting everyone involved and having an input into the way the team works. Established rules of operating can then be used to help any new team members who join later.

Should a meeting not be possible, the whole area of working and building trust becomes more challenging – technology being a poor substitute for face to face discussions.

BUILDING TRUST

BUILDING TRUST

THE BIG CHALLENGE

A challenge for any virtual team is how to build trust between people who may not know each other and rarely meet.

Trust:
- Is vital for any team to be successful
- Helps collaboration through the sharing of knowledge and experience
- Encourages people to be open and honest with each other
- Promotes new ideas, risk-taking and allows people to go beyond their comfort levels
- Is a way of developing co-operation

Trust exists when people deliver their promises and commitments to team members, share information and demonstrate a level of competence.

An initial meeting gives you the chance to start building relationships and trust. This is, however, the easy part: building on it and making it work from a distance are more demanding.

BUILDING TRUST

ISSUES FOR VIRTUAL TEAMS

These include:

- You not knowing your colleagues except as a voice at the end of a phone or a name on an email

- Having little or no prior history of working together

- Lack of face to face communication means you cannot pick up non-verbal cues. As a result it's difficult to anticipate people's reactions to particular situations

- Time pressures put the emphasis on achieving the task at the expense of developing relationships and trust

- Having limited contact due to working across time zones

The bottom line is that teams need people to co-operate with each other to be successful. If you don't trust your fellow team members, then you may well be reluctant to help and assist them.

BUILDING TRUST

NECESSARY BEHAVIOURS

The basis for trust comes from team members being:

- Clear about what has to be achieved
- Competent
- Skilled at communicating with each other
- Prepared to listen, telling the truth
- Reliable: meeting commitments and promises
- Calm at times of difficulty or crisis
- Positive even when things go wrong or faced with criticism

Above all, trust comes from what you do over a period of time – the actions you take – and not simply from saying the right words. **Trust takes a long time to develop, can be lost in a moment and should not be taken for granted.**

DEMONSTRATING TRUST

You can show that you are trustworthy by:

- Being consistent in your behaviour to other team members

- Being seen to be fair

- Giving recognition when it's deserved – not trying to take the credit for the work of others

- Promoting your team to others, not simply promoting yourself

- Anticipating problems and being proactive

- Respecting others and dealing with any conflicts you may have in private and not in public

- Being positive even when things go wrong. Mistakes will occur: acknowledge what happened, talk it through, *learn* and move on

- Not blaming technology for communication failures – virtual teams are about people and relationships, not technology

- Being a good example for people to follow

POSITIVE STEPS

As already mentioned, developing trust is much more difficult if people have never met.

- If a meeting is not possible, try to set up a session using a combination of email, your team website and video conferencing to share personal details and interests

- In the early stages, put your efforts into getting to know each other socially, rather than focusing totally on work

- Be prepared to raise the subject of 'trust' and what it means. Work at getting a common understanding

- As a team, the more involvement and input you have into what you do and how you do it, the greater will be the chances of trust developing

POSITIVE STEPS

- Treat each other with respect at all times
- Be prepared to give people the opportunity to demonstrate that they can be trusted. Don't make snap judgements about your colleagues
- Don't hesitate, however, to speak to people who don't keep their promises
- If you suspect a colleague is not being honest or is keeping information back, have a word with them in private
- If your agreed standards or rules aren't working, then do something about them. They may need adjusting

BUILDING TRUST

SWIFT TRUST

Researchers who have studied how trust develops suggest that it increases as people learn:

- The benefits to be gained from trusting each other and the penalties for not doing so
- Who to trust and the degree to which they can predict colleagues' behaviour
- The shared beliefs and values of the group

A lot of virtual teams are, however, temporary in nature (eg construction projects, films/theatre, those dealing with accidents or disasters), with tight timescales in which to operate and achieve goals.

Myerson, Weick and Kramer *(Trust in organisations)* have argued that a different form of trust is needed in these temporary teams – one that they called 'swift trust'. The targets and timescales don't allow the luxury of developing relationships over time. Members must move quickly to set goals and operate as if trust was already in place.

BUILDING TRUST

SWIFT TRUST

Often, having to *hit the ground running* is enough to focus people's attention on developing a way of working and learning to trust. In these situations where speed is critical, trust is developed by:

- Focusing on the goal and timescale

- Placing emphasis on doing and involving, rather than relating to each other

- Concentrating on the task and/or process rather than on people

- Respecting people's professional skills and specialisms (individuals don't have to prove themselves to other team members)

- Sorting out problems and difficulties quickly and making decisions on the spot

- Having a competent leader who picks reliable people and makes sure that they have all they need to perform, thus avoiding arguments over resources – a sure sign of lack of trust

NOTES

MAKING TECHNOLOGY WORK FOR YOU

MAKING TECHNOLOGY WORK FOR YOU

WHERE ARE YOU STARTING FROM?

Virtual teams have been made possible owing to developments in technology.

We are all making much more use of email, phone and internet in our everyday lives. However, do we really know what such technology can do and use it to its full potential?

A tip is to find out what people know and can do early on in the life of any team. It may be that increasing people's knowledge and skill base needs to be a priority for your team.

The choice of technology – what you have and how you will use it – is a critical decision.

MAKING TECHNOLOGY WORK FOR YOU

THE PURPOSE OF TECHNOLOGY

You want technology to help you as a team:

- Know what's happening at all times
- Understand where your contribution fits into the *big picture*

- Get in touch with each other quickly, as and when required
- Share information and get answers to questions

MAKING TECHNOLOGY WORK FOR YOU

REAL TIME & ASYNCHRONOUS

There are two types of technologies that you can use.

Real time – updating information at the same rate or time as it is received, eg:

- Instant messaging
- Chat rooms
- Whiteboard
- Video conferencing
- Audio conferencing
- Email

Asynchronous – not existing at the same time:

- Discussion boards
- File share
- Web share

MAKING TECHNOLOGY WORK FOR YOU

INSTANT MESSAGING

Technology has changed the way we communicate. Emails have replaced letters and the phone offers a range of innovative ways of contacting each other.

Instant messaging (IM) allows you to:

- Create your own team chat room
- Send text notes back and forth to colleagues
- Share links to relevant websites
- Create and share images
- Share files by sending them directly to people
- Keep up-to-date using *real time* or near *real time* information and news

INSTANT MESSAGING – CHAT ROOMS

Chat rooms have become one of the fastest-growing segments of the internet, partly because many young people find them great fun.

Most *chat* is text-based where conversation is typed, with the message appearing immediately on the screen. Increasingly, audio-based chat is being offered, requiring a computer with a microphone and speakers. This allows the potential to chat to your team members while they are online.

MAKING TECHNOLOGY WORK FOR YOU

INSTANT MESSAGING – TEXT

Text messaging is the common name for SMS, Short Message Service. It's ideal for quick messages to people's mobile phones and normally cheaper than a mobile phone call. There's a high probability that your message will be read, and responded to if required.

Texting is:

- Affordable with low or no set up costs
- Simple to use
- Quick, and it is easy to send the same message to several people
- Instant – messages are in most cases delivered in seconds
- Global – SMS text can be sent to almost anyone in the world
- A cost-effective way of keeping your team involved

MAKING TECHNOLOGY WORK FOR YOU

INSTANT MESSAGING

Pros
- Interactive, informal and *real time*
- Helps as a way to check on people's availability
- Enables you to get replies to questions and information for decisions
- Can be more effective than email for resolving issues quickly
- Can be used for one-to-one or conference mode

Cons
- Not all applications will connect with each other – **your team needs to agree on a common system**
- Security, reliability and spam are potential issues and need to be guarded against
- Intrusive into your personal life – does that sound familiar?

MAKING TECHNOLOGY WORK FOR YOU

WHITEBOARD

If you are holding a live session with your team members, whiteboard technology allows you to:

- Produce, present and update graphic information
- Arrange the contents by clicking, dragging, and dropping information on the whiteboard with the mouse
- Write, enlarge, move, cut, copy, paste, delete, group and ungroup items
- Draw freehand, straight lines, squares, circles and highlight items
- Use different colours to represent individual team members' comments
- Review what's been produced and save the contents for future reference

Whiteboards:

- Are ideal for generating ideas and for problem solving sessions
- Allow the person running the meeting (the moderator) to control the layout

It's important though to make sure you check that all your colleagues have access to the same whiteboard technology.

AUDIO CONFERENCING

Audio conferencing is a facility that allows three or more people to be linked together through a telephone call. All the people involved in the conference can hear each other and can also speak interactively. It is sometimes referred to as phone conferencing or teleconferencing.

Audio conferencing is ideal for your virtual team if people are based in different locations and rarely have the opportunity to meet.

However, as with any meeting, they can be seen as a potential waste of time. To make the most of your audio conferences, read the pages that follow on good practice.

MAKING TECHNOLOGY WORK FOR YOU

AUDIO CONFERENCING
GOOD PRACTICE

Nominate a chairman

- This is the person who hosts the conference and organises it.
  It doesn't have to be the leader of your team
- The chairman can also decide who contributes and when

Arranging the conference

- Decide on a time and book the call
- Let people know the date, time, subject(s) to be discussed, phone
  number to call and any PIN number to quote when they enter the conference.
  Don't forget to allow for any time zone differences
- Send a reminder (text, email) the day before the call

MAKING TECHNOLOGY WORK FOR YOU

AUDIO CONFERENCING
GOOD PRACTICE

Start and end times
- The conference begins when two or more people have entered
- To leave a conference, you simply have to put down the phone
- It ends when the last person puts down the phone
- It's possible to involve mobile phones in a conference but the downside is that people may drop out if their connection fails

Maximum number of people
- There are packages that allow 20 or so people to be involved at once
- However, as with a face to face meeting, the more people involved, the harder it is to keep good order when everyone wants to participate
- Managing those inputs can become difficult unless guidelines are laid down and followed. Generally it is better to keep the numbers of participants down if possible

MAKING TECHNOLOGY WORK FOR YOU

AUDIO CONFERENCING
GOOD PRACTICE

Taking part in an audio conference for the first time can be a confusing experience. The absence of eye contact means that certain rules must be followed to avoid confusion and make best use of the time.

These include:

- Welcoming all participants at the start
- Re-stating the purpose of the meeting and the time it will end – a good discipline for any meeting
- Conducting a roll-call to check who's present, as well as to identify participants to one another
- Inviting contributors to identify themselves before speaking
- Asking participants to use their mute button if they are in a noisy environment
- Reminding participants that they must not put the conference *on hold*, as with some systems music will play across the conference!
- Closing with a summary – again, good meeting practice
- Issuing meeting minutes, action points and details of the next audio conference to team members

MAKING TECHNOLOGY WORK FOR YOU

VIDEO CONFERENCING

Advances in technology have opened up the whole area of video conferencing. Gone are the days of shaky camera, poor quality images, expensive and, at times, unreliable equipment. Even so, it pays to do your research and take advice on the best systems to use for your needs.

Today the emphasis is not simply on talking to people, but using technology to work collaboratively with people on documents, presentations and spreadsheets.

You can video conference between two locations, using the web. Video conferencing is similar to television in its use of the visual and audio channels to get its message across. However, unlike television it is interactive and users need to follow some simple rules to make it a success.

MAKING TECHNOLOGY WORK FOR YOU

VIDEO CONFERENCING

TIPS

- Avoid distracting noises such as tapping and whispering, as these will be picked up and can cause a distraction

- Similarly, avoid unnecessary movements as these can be exaggerated on the screen

- Put the emphasis on what you say; try to avoid using gestures to make more of your message

- Look at the camera when you're talking and not at the screen

- Be aware of time delays

- Be patient and wait until others have finished talking before making your point. (While we all too readily interrupt people in face to face meetings, video conferencing makes interruptions stand out, especially where there is a delay due to network connections)

MAKING TECHNOLOGY WORK FOR YOU

EMAIL

Given the explosion in the use of email it seems almost insulting to people's intelligence to write a few pages on its use. However, if you plan to use email as a means of communicating amongst your team, you need to be aware of the potential risks and how they can be avoided.

While emails have the advantage of:

- Speed – with the potential for an instant response
- Direct contact – to the people who matter
- Worldwide applications – again, ideal for virtual teams

They can also cause:

- Confusion – people don't understand what you're talking about
- Offence – when humour is used inappropriately (beware – a potential danger with cross-cultural teams)
- Frustration – with numbers of emails sent and the requests they may contain

MAKING TECHNOLOGY WORK FOR YOU

EMAIL

Common mistakes include:

- Sending too many, copying people in on every issue and overwhelming them with information – relevant or otherwise

- Use of over-complex jargon or language which may be confusing to some of your fellow team members

- Writing as you would speak and not adjusting the content and communication style to both the audience and the technology

- A casual approach to spelling and grammar

Email does not convey emotions nearly as well as face to face or phone conversations. Thus, unless people know you well, they may not be able to tell if you are being serious, happy or funny in what you write, and may misinterpret your message.

MAKING TECHNOLOGY WORK FOR YOU

EMAIL

TIPS

- Don't make email (or any one form of technology) your only method of communicating. You need a mixture in case there are problems
- In the early stages, when your team are coming together, agree a set of rules for handling emails and other technologies (the popular word is *netiquette*)
- Encourage people to share their experiences of using emails in other virtual situations: what has worked, what hasn't. As a result draw up your own list for good practice
- Remember that emails are good for getting people to share what they know and communicating facts. Face to face meetings are important for reaching consensus on complex issues
- Before sending an email, always ask yourself if it is really necessary

MAKING TECHNOLOGY WORK FOR YOU

EMAIL

TIPS

- Establish rules for what is communicated and its importance for your team
- Where possible, try to ensure that you all use the same application
- Avoid the label *Urgent* on every communication. Make the subject clear and indicate if it is for information, discussion, decision and/or action
- Identify standards for replying to emails so as to avoid delay
- Encourage your colleagues to make use of messaging services such as an *out of office* response so that others know when they are not available
- Put in place a weekly update routine. It need not necessarily come from the leader – all members could contribute a few lines on what they have done, any progress made and lessons learnt
- Ring people up. Emailing can take time – not all people are skilled typists. Sometimes it is easier, quicker and cheaper to talk to people direct
- Finally, be aware of any cultural differences between your team members and make allowances for this in both the style and content of your communication

MAKING TECHNOLOGY WORK FOR YOU

EMAIL
GOOD PRACTICE

Avoid crazy deadlines
- Sending an email at the end of the day asking for a reply tomorrow is often unreasonable and can even be impossible, given time zones
- Sending something electronically does not automatically make it a priority for the other person – they may have other demands or be away
- If you need an urgent reply, phone either before or after sending the email

Take care with your tone – avoid 'flame mail'
- 'Flame mail' is email designed to criticise or ridicule the other person. However tempted you might sometimes feel, just don't do it
- Short phrases and language are OK, but check the overall tone
- Observe the rules of good writing and grammar; keep your message as brief as is practicable
- Limit each email to a single topic even if it means sending several separate ones
- Read it through – would you be happy if this was sent to you?
- *Please* and *thanks* add only a couple of words but mean a lot

MAKING TECHNOLOGY WORK FOR YOU

YOUR OWN VIRTUAL COMMUNITY

The technology exists to set up your own dedicated site for team members to interact via internet websites, discussions boards, etc. These are sometimes referred to as online communities – a community being a group of people who share a common interest or goal. On a dedicated site you can:

- Share details of team members including expertise, interests, contact addresses
- Outline your team's plans
- Track progress against deadlines
- Post meeting agendas, supporting information and minutes
- Send messages to the team and between individuals
- Use discussion boards
- Exchange information and ideas through file and web sharing
- Build up your own knowledge bank
- Run live online sessions, etc

For examples of virtual communities go to www.thelearningbusiness.com.

MAKING TECHNOLOGY WORK FOR YOU

YOUR OWN VIRTUAL COMMUNITY

A community will give your team a focal point. It will allow your team to direct the bulk of their conversations away from email and on to a shared workspace.

Your team may need some technical help to set it up. It pays to:

- Be clear about why it's being set up and how it might complement what else you are doing as a team

- Decide who will have access to the site and how to encourage its use

- Check that all team members have adequate computer equipment and internet access to any system you set up

- Give some thought to the features you want to include on your site

- Lay down some ground rules and guidelines for using the community

- Remember that any community needs to be moderated – someone to supervise the site. Training will help develop the skills and experience needed. This includes familiarity with the tools, how a community works and ways of getting the best from it

ROLE OF A MODERATOR

The team leader is the obvious person to act as moderator. However, don't automatically take on the position if there's someone in the team with better skills who is willing to take the job on.

The task of the moderator is to:

- Act as the central point for communication and collaboration
- Regularly update new home pages, new discussion messages, files and web shares
- Arrange online community live sessions and real time instant messaging sessions

By keeping the content lively, fresh and stimulating, the chances of the team remaining interested will increase.

DISCUSSION BOARDS

Discussion boards are held on the web and are a means of allowing your team to discuss and share ideas with each other. Visitors to the board can read any messages that have been posted. New messages can be added at any time.

Discussion boards are usually made up of:

- *Topics* containing messages on a particular subject

- *Threads* around topics of relevance and interest (tip: it helps to summarise **rather than leave them open-ended**)

- *Messages* which are individual contributions to a conversation (like a single email)

MAKING TECHNOLOGY WORK FOR YOU

DISCUSSION BOARDS

BENEFITS

- Discussion boards develop collaboration in a way that encourages people to share thoughts, ideas and experiences as well as challenge what's happening

- Given that they are asynchronous (ie not real time) you can all read what's been posted and join the discussion at any time

- You can make an immediate response, give some thought as to how you might contribute or simply read what's been said

- Discussion boards can be seen as impersonal, with no face to face interaction; they do, however, create a level playing field which allows your quieter colleagues to contribute on an equal basis

Tip
Use discussion boards for stimulating ideas and solving problems, especially where time and distance do not allow real-time interaction.

MAKING TECHNOLOGY WORK FOR YOU

FILE & WEB SHARING

File sharing is literally the sharing of files – in the form of documents or images – between computers connected via a local network or the internet.

This allows you all to have access to a whole range of information that is available online.

Web sharing allows the team to share useful websites.

So, if you are looking for information on a certain topic or have found an item of interest for your team, use file and web sharing. However, check that you are not breaking any laws and always acknowledge the source.

MAKING TECHNOLOGY WORK FOR YOU

SUMMARY

Why does this matter?

- The chances are that the main method of communication for your team will be through technology
- Communication helps build trust
- Email is not the only way – there are many other methods that will help involve everyone and stimulate interest
- Technology can be used to share information; the biggest potential, however, can be gained from using it to develop relationships
- Successful VTs demonstrate a high level of technical expertise
- Technology that engages more senses improves VT performance *(see www.suddenteams.com)*
- As a team leader, you can use technology to monitor individual performance and see who is – and who is not – participating

MAKING TECHNOLOGY WORK FOR YOU

SUMMARY

1. Start by establishing existing knowledge and skills levels. Find out what equipment you each currently use and for what purposes. Bear in mind that people rarely use a product to its full potential.
2. Seek advice as to the best way of integrating technologies. You all may be using different systems.
3. As a leader, consult your team on the best systems to use and get their reactions (though money might be a deciding factor in your final choice).
4. Build in both the costs and time involved in training people, plus technical support for your team. This is often overlooked.
5. Make sure you agree technical standards and ways of working.

Once you've set everything up, be prepared to evaluate how it is working and make any changes that may be necessary.

FINAL THOUGHTS

LEAD, DON'T MANAGE

In the absence of daily face to face contact, leadership of the team becomes critically important. As the leader, help your people deliver and be seen to be contributing by making it clear what's expected of them and where they fit in, and by giving help and support.

- Keep in contact with people on a daily or regular basis. Take note of what is happening. If there's a problem, work with people to deal with it and get them re-focused and back on track

- Don't be seen to have grudges or favourites. Promote your team in public and support them in the face of any criticism

- Build up other people's trust in you by acting as a role model and meeting any promises you make

- Rotate the leadership as a way of using or developing colleagues' skills and acknowledging their capabilities

- Finally, if things go wrong, look at yourself first

DON'T RUN AWAY FROM CONFLICT

No team ever achieved success without the occasional disagreement.
Conflicts may arise around how the team's task should be tackled and amongst
yourselves when personalities clash.

- If your team is to be successful then 'task' conflict needs to be encouraged
  as a way of getting you all to share your ideas and experiences
- Ensure that any conflict doesn't get personal and lead to falling out
- Remember that working in a virtual set up makes it harder to restore
  damaged relationships – any well-meaning attempts to repair
  situations with emails can make matters worse
- The more you trust each other, the more you will be able
  to have disagreements yet still retain respect
- You all have a role in bringing conflicts out
  into the open rather than ignoring them

FINAL THOUGHTS

COMMUNICATE, COMMUNICATE, COMMUNICATE

In the absence of regular social contact other ways of promoting team development and relationship building need to be found. As a team see if you can come up with ideas to make this happen.

- Work out a way of letting each other know when you are available, where you will be and how you can be contacted
- Talk to each other outside of any formal meetings
- Vary the communication medium
- Make allowances for any cultural differences that may exist when you are communicating

IT'S ALL ABOUT PEOPLE

Don't fall into the trap of getting obsessed with the technology; people make teams successful and not machines. Your contact with each other may be remote, but always remember that you are dealing with human beings. You each have feelings, needs, hopes and aspirations that you want met.

- Treat people with respect, involve them, take care with your communications, don't be afraid to ask for feedback
- In face to face teams demands would not be made or changes imposed, without involving people. Don't change just because you are working at a distance
- Instead of emailing, pick up the phone and talk to people
- Don't undervalue the impact of saying *thanks* to people – not only when things go well but especially in difficult times. It's easy to feel isolated and your efforts ignored
- Finally, enjoy it – **virtual working is here to stay**

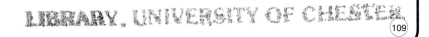

FURTHER READING

There are plenty of good books about virtual teams. Try:

Virtual Teams: People Working Across Boundaries with Technology
Jessica Lipnack and Jeffrey Stamps
Published by John Wiley & Sons (September 2000)

Mastering Virtual Teams: Strategies, Tools and Techniques that Succeed
Deborah L. Duarte and Nancy Tennant Snyder
Published by Jossey-Bass (September 2000)

The Distance Manager: A Hands On Guide to Managing Off-Site Employees and Virtual Teams
Kimball Fisher and Maureen Fisher
Published by McGraw-Hill Education (September 2000)

Virtual Teams That Work: Creating Conditions for Virtual Team Effectiveness
Cristina B. Gibson and Susan G. Cohen
Published by Jossey-Bass (February 2003)

Useful titles in the Pocketbook series include *Assertiveness*, *Networking*, *Cross-cultural Business*, *Cultural Gaffes*, *Influencing*, *Coaching* and *Diversity*.

The internet is a good source of information on a range of topics related to virtual teams. There's a mixture of research based sites, together with those detailing people's experience as leaders or team members.

About the Author

Ian Fleming MA DMS Dip Ed
Ian works with individuals and teams helping them achieve
results by raising their level of performance and confidence.

Contact
Should you want to talk to Ian about his ideas and approach,
contact him at;
'Summer Bank'
38 Abbey Road
Llandudno
North Wales LL30 2EE
Tel 01492-877539
e-mail ian@creativelearning.uk.com

Thanks
To the many virtual teams that I have worked with across the world and for the lessons learnt. To
Pete Butler for his help with technical information and Barry Peel for his comments, insights and
humour, without which this book would have been virtually impossible.

ORDER FORM

	No. copies

Your details

Name _____

Position _____

Company _____

Address _____

_____

_____

Telephone _____

Fax _____

E-mail _____

VAT No. (EC companies) _____

Your Order Ref _____

Please send me:

The Virtual Teams _____ Pocketbook ☐

The _____ Pocketbook ☐

The _____ Pocketbook ☐

The _____ Pocketbook ☐

The _____ Pocketbook ☐

Order by Post

MANAGEMENT POCKETBOOKS LTD

LAUREL HOUSE, STATION APPROACH,
ALRESFORD, HAMPSHIRE SO24 9JH UK

Order by Phone, Fax or Internet

Telephone: +44 (0)1962 735573
Facsimile: +44 (0)1962 733637
E-mail: sales@pocketbook.co.uk
Web: www.pocketbook.co.uk

MANAGEMENT POCKETBOOKS